Pebble® Plus

SPORTS STARS

STARS OF

STOCK CAR RACING

by Mari Schuh

Consulting Editor: Gail Saunders-Smith, PhD

CAPSTONE PRESS
a capstone imprint

Pebble Plus is published by Capstone Press,
1710 Roe Crest Drive, North Mankato, Minnesota 56003
www.capstonepub.com

Library of Congress Cataloging-in-Publication Data
Cataloging-in-Publication Data is on file with the Library of Congress.
ISBN 978-1-4914-0593-2 (library binding)
ISBN 978-1-4914-0627-4 (ebook pdf)

Editorial Credits
Erika L. Shores, editor; Juliette Peters, designer; Eric Gohl, media researcher; Tori Abraham, production specialist

Photo Credits
AP Photo: Autostock/Nigel Kinrade, cover; Newscom: Icon SMI/Brad Schloss, 13 (top), Icon SMI/David Hahn, 9 (top), MCT/Jeff Siner, 19 (bottom); Shutterstock: Action Sports Photography, 1, 7 (all), 11 (all), 15 (top), 21 (top), Beelde Photography, 15 (bottom), 17 (all), 19 (top), 21 (bottom), David Huntley Creative, 5, Doug James, 9 (bottom), Photo Works, 13 (bottom)

The author dedicates this book to Alex and David Schuh.

Note to Parents and Teachers

The Sports Stars set supports national social studies standards related to people, places, and culture. This book describes and illustrates stars of stock car racing. The images support early readers in understanding the text. The repetition of words and phrases helps early readers learn new words. This book also introduces early readers to subject-specific vocabulary words, which are defined in the Glossary section. Early readers may need assistance to read some words and to use the Table of Contents, Glossary, Read More, Internet Sites, and Index sections of the book.

Printed in China.
032014   008085LEOF14

⭐ Table of Contents

Start Your Engines!

Stock cars zoom around

a big track. Fans pack stands.

They cheer for their favorite

NASCAR drivers.

NASCAR stands for the National Association for Stock Car Auto Racing.

Kyle Busch

Top stock car driver Kyle Busch holds many records. In one season he won 24 races in NASCAR's three series.

Dale Earnhardt Jr.

Fans love Dale Earnhardt Jr.

He was named the Cup Series

Most Popular Driver 11 times

in a row.

Jeff Gordon

Jeff Gordon has won 87 Cup races. He is in third place for the most wins in NASCAR history.

Kevin Harvick

Driver Kevin Harvick has won
the Coca-Cola 600 twice.
The 600-mile (966-kilometer)
race is the longest in NASCAR.

Jimmie Johnson

Jimmie Johnson is a record holder.

He is the only driver to win

five Cup Series titles in a row.

14

Kasey Kahne

In his first year driving in NASCAR, Kasey Kahne earned a top honor. He was named NASCAR's Rookie of the Year.

17

Matt Kenseth

The Daytona 500 is NASCAR's most famous race. Matt Kenseth is one of 11 drivers to win the race twice.

19

Danica Patrick

The first woman to earn a pole position at the Daytona 500 was Danica Patrick. She qualified for the 2013 Daytona 500 with the fastest time.

The pole position is the best spot at the start of a race.

Glossary

Cup Series—NASCAR's top series for pro stock car drivers; the series is now called the Sprint Cup Series

Daytona 500—NASCAR's most famous race; the Daytona 500 takes place in Daytona Beach, Florida

NASCAR—the National Association for Stock Car Auto Racing

qualify—to earn a starting spot in a race by completing timed laps

record—when something is done better than anyone has ever done it before

rookie—a driver in his or her first year of pro stock car racing

series—several races that make up a season

stock car—a race car that looks much like everyday cars that people drive

title—an award given to the champion of a sport

Read More

Donovan, Sandra. *Cool Stock Car Racing Facts.* Pebble Plus. Cool Sports Facts. Mankato, Minn.: Capstone Press, 2011.

Howse, Jennifer. *NASCAR Sprint Cup.* Pro Sports Championships. New York: AV2 by Weigl, 2013.

Wilson, Walt. *Jimmie Johnson.* Superstars of NASCAR. New York: Gareth Stevens, 2011.

Internet Sites

FactHound offers a safe, fun way to find Internet sites related to this book. All of the sites on FactHound have been researched by our staff.

Here's all you do:

Visit *www.facthound.com*

Type in this code: 9781491405932

Super-cool stuff!

Check out projects, games and lots more at
www.capstonekids.com

23

★ Index

Word Count: 180
Grade: 1
Early-Intervention Level: 18